THESE LATEST
Apocalypses

THESE LATEST
Apocalypses

Jason Montgomery

New York

A special thanks to The Parliament Literary Journal,
NatureCulture's Root to Seed: Anthology of
Native/Indigenous Writers Living in the Northeast,
Meat for Tea, Cape Cod Review, Genre: Urban Arts,
Cosmonauts Avenue, iō Literary Journal,
The Dewdrop, Rust and Moth, Passengers Journal,
swifts & slows, Broken Lens Journal, Beyond Words,
& SoFloPoJo - South Florida Poetry Journal,
where some of these poems first appeared.

Cover art: *7th & Alamitos*, Jason Montgomery

ARTEIDOLIA PRESS
New York

arteidolia.com/arteidolia-press

First Edition
Library of Congress Control Number: 2023915589
ISBN: 979-8-9889702-1-7

To my mother & sister:
Without you, I wouldn't be here to write these poems.

And to Alex Woolner:
Thank you for being my coffee-mate.

THESE LATEST APOCALYPSES

My window wears a mask

My open kitchen window takes long, deep breaths
Through its mask material, then rests,
Longing for the next moment
When I will close it off
To shelter in place
Or places hidden now
In the broad outside
Skies of blue
Tangled with
white.

Urchin

We spent the afternoon laughing,
As we Slipped and stumbled over the rocks along the Central
Coast.
Every few seconds, we stopped
To smash purple sea urchin with scuba hammers.

On the rocks
They shattered like tea cups
Leaving blobs of yellow-orange flesh to mark our path.

Flocks of seabirds joined our peregrination
Scoters, Loons, Grebes and shouting Gulls
Dashed from kill to kill
Feasting on the remains.

There was simple joy in it.
We competed to see who could cull the most
Promised dinner to the winner.

When the sun grew too hot
We stripped off our clothes,
Left them scattered along the shore
And dove into the waves.

We should have met a kelp forest.
Gently swinging blades and stems.
Schools of Garibaldi and Yellowtail.
Octopi with questioning eyes.

Instead there were just more urchins.
They have taken the forests.
They stretched out to the horizon.

Unit 268

To whom it may concern,

I left you this poem tucked into the padlock on my storage unit, which I lost today.

I hope when you find it, you don't stop to read these words before cutting through the shackle. Use your bolt cutters to cut this poem so its locking pawl is useless, and its lock body falls clattering to the asphalt. Kick it aside with your instep into the shadows laced with fluorescent light cast by the planter filled with coke bottles, used gum, and three flowers.

****

For Maria, who cleans the building,
  I am sorry to have littered this poem. I know that too much of your time is spent dealing with the mess left by others. If you can do me a favor and tear what you find in half, putting one half into the trash bag, but rolling the rest between your palms into a tight ball that you throw over the ˆΩback fence into the afternoon, I would be grateful.

I know this is asking a lot, considering every time you saw me, I forced you to ask me for the late rent. We both knew I had no intention of paying.

****

Dear Puppet,
When you find this wadded ball of poetry during your daily trip through the alley on your daughter's bike, take a moment to forgive me for not coming back, then tear this poem in half.

I know you will want to chew both halves to make double sure it can't be read again, like you did on the yard a thousand times, but please let the Santa Ana winds take one half away before you do what you do with the other.

****

To you, dearest Santa Ana Winds,
I hope this poem finds you well, and that you will be gentle with
us this year because no matter what they say, or if they call you
a devil wind after yet another wildfire,
 I will always love you.

With love,
The Former Owner of Unit 268

Wood Parts Earth

Post holes mile upon mile
Connected by borders of steel frames
Grown in the soil of distrust
Protecting no one here
From the rumored dreams
Of no one there.
Boundaries
Standing
Still.

Ants
Gathered
Under trees
With a broken
Twig you found behind
The home team dugout bench
Then kept in a glass test tube
I carried with me in the sky
Tied in my hopes for a better life.

To the Witnesses

I'm not the hero of my story for surviving it
At best I was another witness to it

There are people who saw most of my addiction for what it was
–My own private apocalypse–
My breaking.
Those witnesses saw the hurried yellow lines
where I glued myself together every day
So I could break in new and different places.

They could not have seen my smallest still cherished moments
The flutter of drying laundry out the train window as I left
Union Station
The reds, yellows, and pinwheeling metallic sunlight on cheap
toys on a street vendor's cart
The smell of roasting corn in the evening cutting through the
numbness,
The first sip from the mouth of a cooler damp glass coke bottle

Sharing these moments feels like a betrayal.

Ignoring them feels like sin.

Things Left on the Beach

Huntington Beach has titular tides
The first happens long before dawn
It'll come high but nowhere
Not wetting the pier's toes
With barely the strength
to wash ashore
All that I
Ever
Lost
Found
among
the damp sand
browning salt foam
bits of broken shell
sea glass worn smooth and dim
bleached cigarette butts
I see our memories of then
Looking new and fresh from the water
Not yet drying in the morning breeze
that comes in with the tide
pushing the heat and salt east
on the tributary
streets and sidewalks
seasoning them
with moments
both then
Now
You
and I
are salt
left at the last
high tide line
dried by the wind and sun
forgotten by the churning.
Coating the bodies of others
As we try to return to the sea.

Cookie Recipes

Chris told me he needs to get his diabetes under control as we set out the chairs for the Tuesday night N.A. meeting.

He actually said his doctor told him his new HIV medication means he won't die of AIDS, so he better get his diabetes under control.

We laughed at the idea that after all these years, the virus wouldn't get him, but he was going to get got by a cookie.

If it was double chocolate chip, it would be a black-on-black-on-black crime;
Oatmeal raisin would be a car accident with Subaru;
Gingersnap would be a hate crime.

We finished setting out the chairs and preparing the room, laughing like soldiers leaving a warzone for the last time.

Every now and then, he still texts me a new cookie.

We make these jokes on the Kaposi's sarcoma-covered backs of our dead friends.

I think they would understand.

Wood

You race far ahead through the cleared woods
Carried by the branches of your youth
Speeding to your potential
Over fallen pine needles
And the ripe acorns
I stop to gather
As tokens
Of our
time.

Underbelly/3 Hours until Closing Time at Velvet Nation, 1998

She has a face like a punk rock song,
A name she doesn't use at night,
And 3 hours left on her shift in the 60-60 cage before she can go home,
Take off her tits,
Put her Face back in its box,
And pass gas like she wants.

Chuey says: "She's a good dude", because she always has that white blown glass pipe in her purse.
The bar backs know they never have to roll a joint from a bar napkin.

She kisses his forehead with a laugh and honest affection,
Despite their encounter in the walkin last spring,
A month before he brought his family back up from Mexico City.

And the Skyline drips drops,
I wonder,
As eyes wander,
Up her right thigh.

Waiting for the Calm That Comes After

There isn't a crowd gathered to watch the three police officers
Failing to hold her arms, ripping her shirt,
Nor preventing her skirt from climbing up her kicking legs,
Showing the tip of her wagging penis.

Before this is over they'll push her head against the sidewalk
And the blood from a gash above her right eye won't be washed
off until the morning.
Her left shoe will lie in the gutter until next week.

In two weeks she will be back waiting to use the showers.
The county hospital stitches will have puckered in purple and blue
But the black eye will have faded.

Right now though she'll hold her ground.
In the now I hope she will give up,
because I need an outfit from the needle exchange,
and have no resistance left.

From across the street I wait for her to lose.

The Blue Line Poet

If you ever get the chance to hear the Poet on the Blue Line from Long Beach to Downtown LA, you won't be disappointed. I mean you will be disappointed by the quality and the pornography of their work. However, if you are one for quality and pornography, or even quality pornography for that matter, you probably don't ride the Blue Line from Long Beach to Downtown LA.

The Poet always gets on at the Compton station. Their readings last to 103rd with the occasional encore to Firestone. They read with aggression borrowed from the rattle and waving of the train car's divide. They read with a love for verse leaning into the long, slopped turns taken too fast by a driver looking to make up time. He rhymes the quick jerks and pops of rocks placed on the tracks by children. His meter is steady. Always out of time against the click-clack of wheels on rails. He doesn't borrow rhythm.

They fight against train sounds everyday.

rattles
metal on metal
crackles from the overhead line
Clip-clock-clop of rail ends

Stutter stops
Horn blare
Chattering shouts
Snores
Coughs.

Their words are heard.

I can't think of the last time I wanted to be seen by anyone.

I can't remember the last time I felt moved enough by my own poems to spend $2.25 to shout them to the uncaring.

Salton Sea

A staggering billboard welcomes visitors to Bombay Beach.

Evaporated salt.
Dead fish.
toxic wind.

This whole place is a broken hand mirror
Turned into an inland lake
Casting back an image of myself.

I am too numb to see.
My decisions are as toxic as the wind off the playa.

Chemily

My grandmother told me ants built the world.

The Chemily. Deep underground.
Little People.

My son gathered the Little People in a discarded water bottle he
found by the park's trash can.

And I try to remember the words to Sweetness Follows.
He will take them back to his mother's house and try to create a
world to watch over.

Driving lessons at the end of the world

I taught my son to drive on the same desert roads I learned on.
The empty nowhere places we both love best,
passed the last of the irrigation canals
And just beyond the green alfalfa fields.

When I was learning my uncle would slap my leg hard if I forgot
the clutch before the brake.
The red welt fingerprints would lay one over the other on my
right thigh
Reminding me for days after that my mistakes.

My son learned to drive on an automatic transmission.

Regardless, he made fewer mistakes than I did at his age.
He has been this way since he was small.
Capable

I abandoned teaching him halfway through the lesson.
He doesn't need me anymore.

Instead, I was content to sit with the window open, and the
radio playing
Quietly watching him decide which road to follow, or which
turn to take
That would lead us to a destination we didn't have.

He took us to the edge of the dying lake where our people
once built fish traps,

Then to start of the dunes where honey pot ants nest,
Across the salt flats to the mountain of obsidian,
And over to the boiling mud pots with its precious clay
Before the sun started to set and we headed home.

This latest apocalypse

My auntie is prepping for this latest apocalypse.
Laughing, she references the current Russian president
alongside Serra, Burnett, and Cortés.
Just another in a long list of apocalypse men.

She asks if my brother sent me Potassium iodide yet.
He has some left over from when his thyroid was removed 15
years ago.
He told her she will need to take one a day once it all starts.

It is just one of the apocalypse instructions she's written on
pink card stock from her scrapbooking supplies in her quick
and tight handwriting.
They sit by the computer she doesn't really know how to use in
her little office.
There is also one that says: "Close Yahoo. Open Google Mail
(Gmail) account. Better?"

In her spare room,
the one my sons call their bedroom,
She has me assemble a wire baker's rack
That she purchased from Costco.
Her supplies are cans of pinto beans,
powdered Ensure,
corn tortillas and one bottle of Chick-fil-A sauce.

Over dinner at La Fonda when I ask her for her plan
Once all the food is gone,
Or if there is no power during the summer
when the heat reaches 120 degrees.

She simply says,
with a laugh,
that I'd know from the other side of the world,
"I will live or I will die just like all the rest."

Poem like a Body

//The wrinkles and runs have become more pronounced//less uneven//more perfect for their imperfection//more widespread//covering the totality of my excuses//like glaze before firing//Like a quiet night//this poem is my body

\\I miss lying on the living room floor on Thursday nights\\ I miss the smell of cigarette smoke hanging on the morning air \\feeling really bad only to get over it once the afternoon sun comes through the side window\\being skin and bones one day\\being ready ready\\

//This will be the better year//we will finally make a little money//finally paint the hallway//finally fix this poem that is a body//finally fix this body that is a poem//finally fix the doorbell//this will be the best year

\\There is hand sanitizer in all the cars \\crumbled and stained paper masks in all our coat pockets\\I cried last night at the end of an end\\the last episode of a show we only watched because we had run out of things to say\\this poem took years to write \\it's still not done.

Half Memory

Hot
Clean dust,
Bleach with starch,
Burnt fields, cow shit
And forgotten days.
You sleep safe in these smells
Among awkwardly long limbs
Is a blanket from my lived youth
And a half memory we now share.

A Weekend on Catalina Island

The fraying hem of my cut-off jeans attracts garibaldi, blue
perch, and the occasional lazy sheephead - more curious about
the swirl of fish I attract than my clothes, skin, or hair.

My arms, legs, chest, and lungs are still strong. My skin is even
brown and only carries the scars I came by honestly.

I am at the center of a spiral fluttering with yellow, blue, orange,
red, and gray fish. When dragged ashore, they look so alien;
here in their world, they look so much more than alive. I can see
the rays of sun cutting through the prism of breaking waves
high above me.

The sound of those waves doesn't carry. Only their gentle
rocking makes it here, moving the towers of kelp and lace of
the sea fans. The only sounds are the ones I brought with me.

Waiting for everything

I will not write a poem about the death of my first child.
Some losses are simply the end of all before and after,
A single point of nothingness,
That waits for you to let go and surrender,
Joining its everythingness.

My son's red hair

Last night my son didn't believe as an infant he had red hair.

I dug through my piles of papers, and doom-boxes
Trying to find photos from his first few days of life.
Those days when his eyes couldn't focus,
And he looked like a small old man.
When we would wake up at 4 AM to feed
And watch Buffy the Vampire Slayer.

My son came screaming into this world
With hair so bright crimson
Even after the nurses had taken him
Pink, purple, and crying,
To wash his mother's body from him
I thought his head was stained with her blood.

He waited with the patience of a teenager
To see his first moments.
Only to realize there was nothing to find.
Their absence is another disappointment
He accepts with the same quiet resolve
As all the rest.

The Half things

I tell my partner that I need ten minutes. That I can't find the remote. Or I forgot to pay this bill or that. We tell each other we love us day and night. The simple statements of a shared life. I don't know if I ever mention that I hate the noise of my own breathing right before I fall asleep or that I don't think I like to listen to the radio in the car anymore. Or that most days my antidepressants give me the thinnest of paper wings.

Why complicate the quiet calm of a shared life, I tell myself?

These aren't hidden things.
Just the blue inside things.
The half things.
The me things.

Peace Interrupts

Not every moment is a horror.
Sometimes joy floats on a puddle
moving like street oil rainbows
after a brief warm rain.
Peace can interrupt
euphoria
long enough
to stop
doubt.

For Sacred 7up

Yarrow doesn't grow in concrete cracks,
nor do citrus trees,
nor are eucalyptus tall timber native,
nor are poultices possible from plastic bags,
recycled cans, glass bottles, or treasure trove copper pipes.
Daycare diseases can't be cured through 405 freeway sweat
houses.

Cartwheeling black mold murals trap houses,
but not hideaway holes with all-patched cracks.
All those notes of overpass MUSTIC can pipe,
or prosper through the fallen boughs of county-cut trees.
I can carry home your brown bags,
but you're too tired to care if I walk on plants now more native
than native.

My fear of the lack of PTO is entire and native.
With 16 thousand in parking space houses,
and more to lose than can fit in 3 bags,
or less to gain from once again falling through the cracks,
I know still days don't grow on trees.
So I shuffle on, stuffed like an overflow drain pipe.

Can I clear that pipe?
Push through the tar and ash now caked native,
or see through the commercial medical trees,
but still, I'll not see the forest from the track houses.
My sacrilegious self is not the only thing now with cracks.
By Thursday, my eyes are just an adornment for my bags.

Two shots in the stratosphere ain't junk bags,
just enough now to fill a glass pipe,
and you'll wonder why I can't hear anymore through the cracks,
but deep desire for a clean spirit is native,
or it was until white sage gave way to project houses.
Only sacred 7up flows from the sap of palm trees.

No one ever told me the danger of catching shade from embellishment trees.
Now my heart rests among orange highway crew trash bags,
and I dream of sterile white houses,
or at least a different flow to this pipe.
I realize then that sickness is now the only native,
then with no resolve, I fall under the weight of my own cracks.

When my time comes, I'll lie in the overgrowth of telephone line trees.
My funeral dress will be faded chip bags.
My eulogy will be the lingering lemon scent of others' clean houses.

Earth and Stone

The weight of earth and stone in our hands
Is the same whether filling or
excavating these graves.
The weight this unearthing
will lift from our hearts
is like mountains
or planets
carried
forth.

A Letter to My Ex-wife re: Your Continued Existence

This morning, the kids' stepmom shared a TikTok with The
Mountain Goats in it,
No Children to be exact.
Maybe you've seen it.
I don't know.

I know when I first played Tallahassee for you in January of 2003,
You didn't care for the tone and tenor of John Darnielle's voice.
You hated it, in fact, and asked me why I wanted to listen to him
whine-yelling
About divorce.

Now it's nearly 20 years later,
And I'm wondering just how we didn't take that as a sign.
I guess it would have helped if I mentioned
How much The Mountain Goats meant to me.

We were getting married in the Spring.
I was already hoping you'd die.
I hoped we'd both die.
I guess it resonated with me.

You never held back your loves from me.
I knew you loved Ringo, though no one else did,
Or that you loved your pet birds as a child,
Even though they kept committing suicide,
And the sight of their broken beaks and bodies
Haunts you to this day.

I wanted to share John Darnielle with you,
The love I had found on a random Napster
That I still dream was someone
In North Carolina.
Maybe on a mountain.
Maybe a goat.

Seeing your face in my memory now,
I'm sure you thought I was trying to say more than I was,
Which, if I can be honest, I was.

The TikTok is funny, by the way.
You should find it.
People have choreographed a dance
That reminds me of you.

That's not quite right.
It reminds me of me with you.

Missing Time

The day I died, I woke up to a nurse putting a plastic hospital bracelet on my wrist.

I didn't wonder where I was.

Instead, I tried to figure out how they had managed to get my limp and heavy body out of the small room in my attic, passed the clutter and trash I filled my room with, down the stairs that were not up to code, and out the front door.

I still don't know.

I didn't know I died, not at first.
No one will tell you right away.

The doctor asked me if I had taken anything they should be aware of,
if I knew what happened to me,
or if I had a history of cardiac events.

It's a game of two truths and a lie.

After the tests were run,
and the doctor was reasonably confident
I would only die once that day,
She told me my heart had stopped.

She wasn't sure for how long.

I will never play saxophone

A friend once told me they could tell me what instrument I
would have played in middle school band. I smiled and laughed
along as they told me I would have played the saxophone. I
didn't have the heart to tell them my middle school didn't have
a band
 – or even instruments.
We had a box.
6'5 and made of steel.
For all the kids that'd take a chunk out of you.

We did have a library,
A small one room trailer filled with donated books,
But it was only open once a week for an hour at lunch.
Wednesdays, mostly.
I found a copy of a graphic novel there.
It was about a blond woman and her beloved monster.
There were boobs in it.
I am still not sure it actually existed.
The librarian was a blond woman who drove in from Seal Beach.
We were her beloved monsters, I think.

We had a LA County Sheriff Deputy
who patrolled the wide asphalt   gaps between
buildings in a squad car.

He was a pacing brown and white cougar
In a zoo where eating the animals was all part of the show.

Nonets

Someone asked me why I write nonets.
I wish I could have explained that
they are how I see the world.
flashes of memory
fleeting clarity
drifting away
bit by bit
Until
Gone.

Folar da pascoa

When I was growing up our neighbor Jessalina used to make
Easter breads with a hard boiled egg in the center.

Folar da pascoa,
but I didn't know
the name
until I was 45
and googled it
for this poem.
The bread is sweet and soft.
The egg is plain and still in the shell.

She would sneak over the brick fence between our houses to
leave the still hot loaves on the window sills
of the bedroom I shared with my two brothers.
I didn't understand why she didn't come to the door.

I get it now.

She came from Portugal. They knew grandpa was from Cape
Verde and treated us all like long lost cousins who had been
taken into the wilds by an ocean storm only to be found again
by the fishing men. We were family to be reminded of man's ways.

Jessalina told me the bread was pregnant with the body of the world.

I felt like a predator.

Her son had died in the long sometime before me. She kept an
identical photo of him in a brown frame in every room. His body
lay in the center of a cemetery in the Whittier hills.

Thursday, April 30th 1992

Morning
John's Hamburgers, 5815 Downey Blvd., was burned to the
ground before the sun came up.

They closed the beaches, but we all still walked to school.
We ate hot lunch under the smoke darkening skies.
100 pre-teens at picnic tables realizing
 we would have 1st period math
on the last day of humanity's last day.

Noon

When big kids at Wilson High poured out into the halls biting,
kicking, and punching any face that didn't look like their own
the schools decided it would be better for us to be at home, or
out in the streets, or on rooftops throwing stones at the police
cars that were everywhere and nowhere all at once.

I remember sitting with my brother on the garage roof trying to
decide if the pyrolysis products drifting on the wind was nearer
or further away than Mr. Kim's store.

He was closed.

David said he and his son were there. He had seen them
although the neon beer signs were off and the Street Fighter
machine was dim.

They stacked bags of rice along the glass front doors, but waved
to him from the dark store.

Evening
The neighborhood men paced the length of the block half
heartedly. They made groups of two, or three, but when four or
more stood for too long one of their wives would break them up.

I don't know where my father was. Working, as likely as not.

At 6 PM the police drove slowly from block to block announcing the curfew.

We had breakfast for dinner. Bacon, pancakes, and eggs.

My mom was grateful the Wonderful World of Disney was only interrupted once by the news.

Night
We slept with all the windows closed.
The sounds of helicopters and sirens seemed no better or worse than any other day.

Mess on the Bathroom Floor

Tomorrow I will try to recall
If I ever told you just how
Little I cared for the mess
you leave in the bathroom
when you change your face
to remove the
mask we both
Deeply
Hate.

Armageddon Games

My son asked me, as we settled into the after-dinner quiet of
being, if, when we played D&D again, could I make an
apocalypse-level event?
He wanted to run to the middle of a magic forest and build a
doomsday bunker from obsidian, so that he could watch the
end of the world from its highest window.

I thought about all the apocalyptic things I could make a game
out of:
Zombie hordes,
Dragon fire,
Or evil wizards.

I thought of all the ends he had lived through in his 12 years:

There have been cataclysms of disease. For three long years,
his little world of lunch boxes, playgrounds, and classrooms
ceased to be, only to be replaced by masked faces, self-tests,
and dead aunties no one seemed to care about.

Smoke days have become an ominous routine, as the wildfire
holocausts relentlessly sweep through California, scorching the
land year after year. The acrid scent of smoke permeates the air,
lingering like a haunting presence.

And amidst the chaos, there echoed the rantings of sad but
powerful men. Their words, fueled by anger and discontent,
reverberated through the air. Their voices carried a certain
charisma, drawing in followers with promises.

His world has ended more times than it began.

I want to build him a tower of obsidian and clay,
A place free of Armageddon games.

A Poem for Easthampton, April 2023

I've wounds inflicted by you.
Black and blue newsprint bruises,
green cactus needle tattoos,
And Poetry paper cuts.

I have self-inflicted wounds.
Brillo pad scratched skin patches
Rubbed raw with hope of hiding
The scars of my brown birth caul.

I was told be more like King.
Keep us, we pray, in perfect peace.
Last I checked they shot him too.
Then put his face on a t-shirt

You're damn right I'm angry

It's a red-skinned Lordean rage.
It's Sun kissed, and sleep deprived,
A rage that's hollow bone deep
Twisted with cell memory

I don't have much more than this.

I have cried red trails of tears
down a face of banished dust.
With no more than a half glance
From you hurried passersby.

Redemption songs have called in
All those standing in earshot
Only to be an off tune
earworm as they walked away

Please hear this fair case for rage.
It's my black burning belief
That voices raised in anger

Will finally be heard true.

Rage is a hope.

Anger is my last screamed prayer.
I bellow it in the dream
You will join in communion
Because you see me as you.

6th and South Spring

I would take my shirt off
To hide my acceptability.
Trying to pass as my authentic self
Dirty, desperate, but not yet dying.

I would walk with my Pendleton in hand
Deeper into the heart of the true LA
Passed Metro Pcs,
tents
The promise of rough trade

To the place where simulacra fights to find its way in on bus
benches
Cigarette ads in liquor store windows
Mcdonald's wrappers used as makeshift toilet paper.

To place where no one knew my name
But everyone still knows the real me

Or at least what's left.

Tomorrow Morning

Tomorrow morning, you will wake up,
When I am just readying for bed.
We will talk briefly about
The small details of life,
Always making sure
We have learned to
share this time
apart
well.

Two by Two by Two

Night is the time for memories\\although nothing good
happens past 2 in the morning\\watching by modern lamplight
\\water light

//two by two by two//warmed in the afterglow of other's
pleasant evenings//cold in the lack between us//the children
call back//they're tied to you through moving shadow//we're
tied to each other through the choices that brought us here//

A Letter to Jade re: Our childhoods

Dear Son,
I want to give you the feeling of being eight,
Because our childhoods are apocalypse.

I want you to have the feeling of sitting in clean pajamas,
In my grandma's back room with the small TV
After coming back from swimming in my Tia's pool
On the hottest day of the desert summer.

I want to show you how my skin
Golden brown, and dripping wet,
Is protection against the high desert sun
And the griddle hot black top,
As my brothers, sisters, and cousins
Make the one block walk back to grandma's
Jumping from tree shadow to tree shadow
Then onto the neighbor's dying grass.

I want you to feel the cold relief
of the central air that is a necessity not a luxury,
Which is such a welcome counterpoint
To the hot dry air outside,
But never so much so that I would sacrifice one forever for the
other.

I want you to smell
mingled of dust, heat, starch,
chlorine, and clean
That was my boyhood.

I need you to forgive me robbing you of yours
as I chased the pale chemical substitute of all of these feelings
For all those years.

That need might be the worst part of me.
The asking for forgiveness
Knowing you now look for all these things I had
But failed to give to you.

In Another Timeline

I can send you a kind of message in a bottle
That I dream is entangled with your old, neon-blue pager.

And you'd receive it back in 1996.

The message from today would tell you that everything is just
okay now.

I wish you nothing but all the years between then and now,
using our old code,

Because that would mean you saw this spelled out in numbers

And knew better.

Changed before you changed.
Changed before I changed.

Making all those 911 messages pointless

Because every tomorrow is already okay.

We would have spent Christmas in Twin Falls, Idaho,

Joking with your daughters and my sons that we were living a
Built To Spill song

Again.

Because everything is okay, I don't think I'll write this message
to you.
Because you are still here and everything is just okay.

This pointless message never gets written.

Your mom still calls me to say they found your body in your car,
And I stand on the shore by the Port of Long Beach,

crying, trying to write you this message.

Court Days

My new shirt still has store folds
With pin holes in the sleeves, back and neck.
My off black slacks need to be back home,
Because my brother works at 3,
And with his violent ways it will be days
Before I could get the explanations to washout.

It took two hours with Windex and a rag to get my shoe stains out.
If the arresting officer doesn't show the prosecution folds.
Of course it's true--Joey's dad used to say it back in the days.
Last time I was here there was a bottle-neck.
But if the docket is right I'm number 3,
Which means I'll have the day to home.

It is a coarse course from here that leads back home.
The 9 blocks to bus stops that sags out.
Dug out the 2 transfers what don't cover Blue Line 3.
But a practiced hand paper folds
And a compassionate driver bends a neck,
At it there in the tip of my fingers from too long sleeves poking out.

Maybe this whole mess'll get thrown out?
I was literally five blocks from home.
That isthmus, channel, pass, that neck,
Which separated house & world from childhood days
My home lays in the Artesian folds
A place that should always be safe even when your strikes are 3.

For luck I could invoke the trinity with movements 3
But the doors are opening out,
And if I don't show than my PD folds.
There is no reason I shouldn't be home.
So I will give up holy moments to save days
Then remind myself to tattoo that prayer on my neck.

I wonder about this hangman's neck.
If given time he could turn it to see passed my number 3?
If he could owl it around to witness my days,
Or witness what has burned out,
Because even the fee will price me out of home
And this shirt can't be returned without its folds.

My face cracks to my neck.
We are postponed until March 3.
There's a lot of wrong that can fill those days.

My Doctor Talked all The Way
Through My Vasectomy

His accent was thick,
Taiwanese.
And comforting for what it was.

He told me baseball stories;
His son as the only Asian kid on the little league team,
They were the Red Sox,
One of six teams in Worcester named the Red Sox.

He told me how he hates American baseball.
A boring game he learned to love
By watching his son become more American.

I could smell my vas deferens burning,
Which should have been a unique odor,
But is really just the same
acrid, sweet, burning tire smell
Of any living flesh on fire.

I wanted to tell him that I hate baseball,
But I love the Dodgers.

I expected the small sections of me he removed
to Bleed Dodger Blue.
But they were nothing more
Than tiny
white
beads.

Oak Tree

They cut down the damn oak tree today
Its hollow became a cancer.
You hated it before then.
In the way you hated
all the things you loved.
The Damn Oak Tree.
It's gone now.
Just like
You.

My Dad called for the Last Time Yesterday

He wanted to tell me there were no Mexicans at his wedding to
my mom.
Expect the Mariachis,

And my Grandma Gomez,
Maybe her sister too,
If she was there than her daughter too,
But she would have been just a baby.

Grandma wasn't Mexican either.
Not really.
She was an Indian.
Pure blood.
She didn't even like Mexicans.

Grandpa Gomez?

He wasn't a Mexican.

He was Portuguese.
[From Cape Verde]

He only pretended to be one so the Census-man didn't think his
black skin made him a black man.

Grandpa Alarcon wasn't Mexican
Tio 'Milo,
Tio Ernest,
Tia Lidia,
Grandma Rita.
Chicano.
Tongva.

So, the only Mexicans there were really the Mariachis.
                                                    And even they were
from Calexico.

I spent too much of 2007 watching The Backyardigans

Pablo is a penguin.
Tasha is a hippo.
Austin is a kangaroo.
Tyrone is a moose.

But Uniqua?

She looks like a ladybug and a meth-head found each other in a
dark, damp field off somewhere in central California, and under
a single crooked tree that once gave fruit, consummate their
union with a 72 hour unlubed fuck-fest only to produce a hybrid
that is all their best features and worst mistakes.

Maybe I'm being unfair.

Janice Burgess, the show's creator, says
Uniqua is a one of a kind unique creature who is based off of
herself as a child. Out of the five, Uniqua is the main character,
and they use her in every story.

I didn't understand until my first child was born how two
totally different beings could come together to produce
something Uniqua.

This is a weird thought for a mixed person to have.

A Uniqua thought.

I think it is because my parents share a sadness that comes from
misaligned expectations that I don't see them as different.

There is a theory that Uniqua is imaginary.

The internet says Tasha and Austin were often too busy to play
with Pablo and Tyrone, so the four of them took advantage of
the empty pink house to create an imaginary friend who would
always be there.

It would dawn on me later that I had done the same thing. I had taken my loneliness and an empty house to imagine my own Uniqua into reality.

When I looked at the face of the small blond child I would tuck into bed each night, I didn't see my own sorrow and loneliness looking back. He was not an empty pink house.

I saw the main character of a story being created as my story was ending.

I would imagine he would be nothing like me. That he would move through the world as his own creature. He would be free of me.

Being honest

I'm being honest
Most of these memories
mold caves
latrine spaces
Lacking oxygen

There are false tunnels
collapsed warrens
where roots of the lies I planted grow into
walls
floors
ceilings

If their trees fall
they would shatter
ripple
across the state

dropping
People
Down

Or maybe the truth would just be blind, hairless, and harmless
things who look alien in the light of day.

The World Softened before my Father Did

He once told me about my great grandfather's guns
And how they had been enshrined with my great-great
grandfather's guns
In a museum in Maricopa county.

An honor for hard men, who've lived then died hard.

He has hard fists.

Chrome six shooters hands.

Even now when I have more gray hair
than he has hair
I fear those hands.

It would be so easy

To paint my own fists gun-metal gray
Then let loose on the hard spots of the world.
Pounding at them   until they softened
Or I break.

Weezer, The Blue Album, Track One

We would sing at the top of our unscarred lungs
Making noise
Through flat tire thumps,
Broken teeth,
Like brakes that make no sense,
And so many other small moments.

Your mom said they found you in your car near Vancouver.
I didn't think to ask if it was BC.

Or if you finally named your dog Jonas.

Life goes by too fast for being so short—like a teenage theme song.

You laughed when I said
I would name my first child
"Wait-there"
—not Wepeel—
Because that was somehow
Better and worse
Then correct.

I wonder, when the time came, if I answered your call
Then came running armed with a cassette tape
Of The Blue Album
And all the love I have
If your batteries would not have run dry.

But workers need to go home
And your name was Jeremy.

My doctor told me that losing weight would be challenging

"You know, because of that 'being-a-brown-person' thing," she said.

She said it would have been my ancestors who stored calories that survived the famines.

The ancestors who could stomach the meager scraps given to them;

The ones that would swallow the moldy bread crusts,
Chew the fatty rotting meats,
Or break their teeth on dried beans.

Those who would stay hungry and moving for days on end,
Having given their food and water to their children,
Willing their legs to move forward,
And their backs not to break under the heat of the sun.

The ones who survived.

I don't know if the math checks out on that.

I do know Grandma was always worried about my weight.

She once told me how much her father's mother sold for.

I am 285 pounds sterling,
and I need to slim down.

Tired

I am tired.

Root to stem, my dogs are barking, my gas tank is empty, I am tired.

I am tired of a 24 hour news cycle.
I am tired of a 30 minute attention span.
I am tired of a 30 second elevator pitch.

I am tired.

I am tired of cries of authenticity from the inauthentic.
I am tired of you trying to explain erasure to me after
having been erased.
It is history, present and future past.

I am tired.

I am tired of my children asking for help to construct a sugar
cube replica of the same Mission that enslaved our ancestors,
stole our name, and then getting a C on the project.
I am tired of just getting it done because of Core Concepts.

I am tired of needing teeth whiter for a smile I don't have.
I am tired of an apple a day.
I am tired of the new Ford Fiesta.

I am tired.

I am tired of the algae blooms, bacteria closures, and trash
pick up days.
I am tired of the 8th largest economy in the World.

I am tired.

I am tired of dream-catchers at gas stations stealing
all the dreams I don't have anymore.

I am tired of John Collier.

I am sun tired.
I am heat tired.
I am snow tired
I am rain tired.

I am tired and I don't want to do this anymore.

Shoplifters Won't Be Prosecuted

The CVS on Long Beach and Del Amo no longer sells toothbrushes.
They keep makeup, baby formula, cigarettes, and cold medicine
behind the counter.
There is a sign on the counter that reads:
"No aceptar efectivo."
When fake ones started rolling in, they stopped accepting cash.

I nudged the man laid out in the parking lot with my heel.
In my defense, I thought he wasn't breathing.
The clerk said he had been in front of the store all day.
The woman ahead of me in line thought he wasn't breathing too.

She said last week there was a man at the bus stop.
He had been there dead for two days
Before anyone did anything.

The kid at the door
Selling band candy in July
Didn't bother lying
About his school anymore.

He hasn't gone since COVID.

He just looked back
At the black Chevy SUV parked
At the back of the parking lot.

I pretended to believe him long enough to say no.
Indigenous Time
I want to be in the memories of my grandmother,
Telling of the years like days.
The precious minutes of birth,
The quiet hours of death,
All those moments adding their song to us.

The Indigenous Time

Counted by the cooking of meat, beans, chilis,
And the pat of tortillas on hands.

I long to be in the now.
Until I feel the flow of the Southern Wind on my back,
Pushing and pushing against all the loose seconds.
Testing the fences like a pack of coyotes.
I scatter.

Running away from the deep desert like rabbits at dusk,
Feeling time melt away into the then of being,
Blistering skin, boiling fat, charring bone,
The white ash of me.

Ibex St. runs on City Time.
Bus schedules, shelter checkouts, free breakfast hours,
and 10 PM quiet times.
Life is dictated on pamphlets and signs,

And Repetition,
And Repetition,
And Repetition.

Life moves at the pace of regulation.

Better Homes

When I was a kid I would dream of sitting in a great wood lined library surrounded by all the books whose titles I didn't know, but I understood to be of merit and import.

I knew there was a whole world of authors that mattered to those that mattered.

In our house the one bookshelf that sat in the living room was filled with Stephen King, the family photo albums, and the Better Homes New CookBook.

On page 514 there is a recipe for Sweet-and-Sour Pork: A combination that can't be beat: deep-fried, batter coated pork with vegetables and pineapple.

Now that I have grown it is good to learn those places I once held in ignorant reverence hold less comfort for me than the Asparagus-Tomato Stir-Fry on page 915.

Dead Places

Love the world's silent, dying places.
Old buildings, dry creek beds, salt flats,
And other moved-on places
Will hold space for when you
Stumble upon them
At moments when
most needed
but not
sought.

Waves

I'll return to Seal Beach.
And sit in the sand by the pier
To watch the waves rolling in.

I'll watch the waves become waves,
Only to crash on the shore,
And become ocean again.

Each unique in form,
But identical in function.

I'll carry their memories with me,
As I too roll away to my own shore,
And rejoice in my return to the ocean.

Morning Routine

Tomorrow will be the day.
I will wake up before my son's first stretches.
Tiny wiggling kicks at nothing
            Followed by his blinkling realization

                                    He is still here
                                    Still living
                        the world did not vanish
                        when he closed his eyes.

I will bathe him in the sink.

                        Watch his tiny fingers clench
                                cascades of water

                Soap bubbles

Before wrapping him in a towel
That could be all the world.

Tomorrow will be the day.

                    We will sit in the morning shadows
                    Cast about through pepper trees

                Avoiding the dew

Speaking our private poems
eating oranges stolen from no one.

                    Tomorrow this world will be gone, replaced
by this morning routine.

Hunting

The first time I returned to you
With the meat of a rattlesnake
You beat me.

You sent me out into the desert
With a rifle, shovel and hoe.

Across creek, dust and sun,
Told to avoid the mountain,
To stray not too far,
Or exist as an alien,
Illegal
In a place exactly like the one I left.

You sent me out
With message, and motive.

Across the highway of black asphalt and yellow paint
And the sun,
And the sun,
And the sun,

Told to hear first with my ears,
then see next with my eyes,
And fight
As the situation deemed necessary.

And the serpent lay in the sun,
And in the sun,
In the sun,
In the sun,
In instinct of care abandoned.

If brush and weeds provided cover,
Cracked earth and stone
An exit,
The ability to walk endlessly avoiding the mountain
At the end of the world.

But rather to both paths end at my ignorance
And inability to let it be.
You will never get this,
But I will still imagine you
Wandering the streets with
Pastels,
Watercolors,
Streams,
Dreams,
And hope for returning to a better land.

Dirt

Park sprinklers go off without warning
Dust covering your pants turns red
Soon you will want to go home
Caking mud on your seat
Back to your mother
Drifting to sleep
Dream of earth
Dream dirt
Dream.

Gardener

I used to stand on the wooden porch of my grandparents' cabin,
smoking with my grandmother,
watching my grandfather
walk along the long, thin rows of his garden.

He would pace the rows of tomatoes,
cucumbers, beans, radishes,
and all the other food crops
grown not for their form but
for their function.

There should have been beauty in that abundance,
instead, his long legs made sorrowful strides
through the green.

When his father died,
His brothers sold off most of the family farm in Arizona.
What wasn't sold, he drank away in time.

The small acre of land on which their cabin sat
had belonged to my grandmother's family,
passed down and protected.

He did his best to will it into being more
by covering most of it in those long, thin rows.
It would always be nothing more than a garden.

And he, nothing more than a gardener.

Where are we?

To be a known entity
> To look me in the face and tell me you don't love me.
>> To look back saying I hate me more than you.

The bits and bobs of living
> The crumbled antiseptic wipes of too many sorrys.

Where are we?
And I'm so sorry.

To be an unknown factor.
> To smell the dry desert grasses.
>> To stare through wildfire smoke.

The jumbled mouthful of this many mini moments.
> The endings of too many first dates.

Where am I?
 And why don't I miss you?

One Night on the way to Temple

It was a heat gun, meticulously laminating fragile wires,
Frayed ends tenderly brought together,
Braided seamlessly, creating an intricate tapestry.

I can still see your face,
Framed by the hues of a sunset,
Illuminated by red lights,
And your car window.

You blurt out subtly anti-Semitic jokes,
That no one should ever hear,
As I drive us to Temple.

I never laughed as hard,
Or as often,
As I did with you.

You are the culmination of my profound epiphany,
Yet another regret,
A braided copper wire surreptitiously borrowing vitality,
Stealing power from the apartment upstairs.

I would have married you,
Carried your next set of children,
Had you not faded like radio waves,
Lost in the depths of the nighttime.

At my daughter's Bat Mitzvah,
You held her hand, interlacing your fat fingers.
Imprinted a shape on flash paper,
Envisioning a future that can't ever come.

You vanished with the flux of my cynicism.
I swore it was perfect.
I'm not sure if I'll recover,
But I'll say it was worth it.

At what point do things overstay their welcome?

Metal Chops Wood

There isn't a trail of dry breadcrumbs
No bit of stale sustenance
Along of the paths of yucca
To guide our way back home.
There is only the
machete wounds
That mark my
Stumble
Here.

Carve
Your name
Deep into
The railroad tie
With a nail from home.
Score it down to the bone.
It will be my reminder
Of pain you suffered at my hand
And the scars you will always carry.

Poet in Residence

My poetry residency at Wistariahurst
Started by calling an ambulance
For the man across the street found overdosing.

In the museum's main gallery,
There was an exhibition of art
from the local elementary school.

I could say I sprang into action,
But that would be a lie.
I did try to shake him.

In honor of Veterans Day,
The walls were covered in crude
but joyful images of fallen soldiers.

He had a small black and white dog.
It barked and nipped at me
when I got too close to him.

In the music room,
They had hung paintings
of a lute, violin, and a piano.

His phone was new
and rang three times.
I didn't answer it.

In the library,
There was a marble bust
of the Bard.

I couldn't stand to be the voice
to bring a stranger
that moment of truth.

The building was donated to the City
by the founding family.
They are long since gone from this place.

How do you tell a voice on the other side
that a loved one
had just disappeared from their life?

I miss the end of the world

I miss the end of the world.

With it the acculturation to the world of the inside. The sleep will keep, surely. Now my wife and sons can spend time learning to take the perfect Polaroid picture or how little known Anunties fall away like like mayflies. There are tracer rounds and combat knife casseroles feeding cities from coast to coast. Radio delays. Dishwasher relays. And Brett Kavanaugh really likes beer.

Still I would like to return to the comfort of sheltering in place in a house that can't hold anymore. My youngest still wears a mask in public. I think it makes him more comfortable to smile behind that illusion of control during the weekly active shooter drills. Run. Hide. Fight.

He tells me as we drive back from the coffee shop, me with more caffeine than sense, and he with a Sunrise Smoothie with no banana, that our dog Fred would be a good Hospital Dog. He could comfort the sick and the dying—The end of the world people—because he is sweet and kind and loves scritches and scratches. He also misses our end of the world bike rides, but that was before Fred.

I want to assure him that there will be another apocalypse soon enough. But he has a math test on Tuesday and I have work.

I don't want to get either of our hopes up.

Time

Go to the places your god won't bother to look.
Walk there, hoof over hoof,
Without malice in your heart
At the smallest of small.
The flow of time is universal
And absolute; regret should be an impossible thing.
In the yard, Puppet smiles.
The joy of 9 years ill spent is weighty,
But still better than nothing.
And I didn't have sex again last night.
It doesn't matter, and matter tells the universe how to move.
I want to move, far from this city, far from anyone who may
know me,
And further from all those who don't.
I should run off into the Salton Sea.
Swim down to the bottom, then bury myself in the salts, metals,
fertilizers, and pesticides.

Puppet knows me better than anyone.
In all the years, only he has seen me struggle out of the desert.
I wonder how many of us are lucky enough to be seen—truly
seen—as he takes my crumbled 10.
At the largest of large, time is an absolute regret.

Acorns

Oak
Acorns
With cracked shells
Littered across
A borrowed nightstand
Are simple mementos.
They are quiet reminders.
Brown, red, golden tiny totems
Of our countless vanished ancestors

www.ingramcontent.com/pod-product-compliance
Lightning Source LLC
LaVergne TN
LVHW041308080426
835510LV00009B/904